Mobile Security & App Protection

How to Keep Your Smartphone, Apps, and Messages Safe from Digital Intruders

By Joe Correa

Published by Live Stronger Faster

This book is for educational and informational purposes only. The author and publisher are not engaged in rendering legal, financial, or other professional advice. Readers should consult a qualified professional before making any financial decisions.

First Edition

Table of Contents

Introduction

In the digital age, your smartphone isn't just a phone. It's your camera, wallet, messaging hub, travel guide, health monitor, and access point to nearly every detail of your personal and professional life. That makes it one of the most attractive targets for cybercriminals, data harvesters, and invasive apps. And while most people lock their front door before leaving home, they rarely apply the same level of security awareness to their most-used device.

This book is your complete guide to defending your mobile life. Whether you use an iPhone, Android, or tablet, this book gives you a clear, easy-to-follow framework to protect your device, your apps, and your data—without needing to be a tech expert. We'll walk through the essential settings, features, and tools that can dramatically reduce your vulnerability, from encryption and app permissions to secure messaging and mobile VPNs.

We'll also shine a light on some of the biggest threats most people don't even realize exist—like fake apps, permission creep, Bluetooth-based attacks, location tracking, and the hidden risks of free Wi-Fi. Each chapter is packed with real-world scenarios, expert tips, and up-to-date security tools you can start using immediately.

By the end of this book, you'll understand how mobile attacks happen, how to recognize warning signs, and most importantly—how to prevent them. You'll learn how to secure your messages, protect sensitive documents, avoid common traps, and take back control of your mobile privacy.

Whether you're a parent, traveler, entrepreneur, freelancer, student, or simply someone who lives life on-the-go, this book will give you the confidence and know-how to keep your digital world locked down—even in the most connected environments.

Let's get started with **Chapter 1: The Real Dangers of Mobile Cybercrime**—and why securing your smartphone is just as important as locking your front door.

Chapter 1: The Real Dangers of Mobile Cybercrime

Most people carry their entire lives in their pocket—but few truly understand the risks that come with it. The smartphone has become an extension of the human brain: it stores our passwords, personal photos, conversations, financial apps, health data, location history, and even biometric identifiers like fingerprints and face scans. That makes mobile devices the most desirable target for cybercriminals, identity thieves, and digital spies. But the threat isn't just about hackers in a dark room writing code. The more serious dangers are often legal, invisible, and built right into the apps we use every day.

Let's start with a fundamental truth: **your phone is always broadcasting data**. Whether it's GPS location, Bluetooth signals, Wi-Fi requests, or mobile advertising IDs, your device constantly communicates with networks, towers, and nearby devices. This stream of data can be collected, stored, analyzed, and sold by app developers, advertisers, or malicious actors. Many people don't realize that even "free" flashlight or weather apps can be embedded with spyware that collects contacts, microphone input, or usage habits—all without raising suspicion.

One of the most common and underreported dangers is

permission creep—a situation where an app initially asks for access to basic functions (like location or photos), but over time requests and accumulates more intrusive permissions. For instance, a simple note-taking app might suddenly want access to your microphone, calendar, or camera. Most users tap "Allow" without understanding the consequences. These permissions can be exploited to eavesdrop on conversations, take photos, or access sensitive files in the background.

Then there's the threat of **fake apps**—malicious software disguised as legitimate applications. These are particularly common on third-party app stores or in countries where Android is dominant. A fake banking app, for example, may look identical to your real bank's app, but instead of helping you log in, it harvests your credentials. Once installed, these apps can operate in stealth mode, intercepting two-factor authentication codes, reading messages, and sending private data to an attacker's server.

Public Wi-Fi poses another huge risk. **Man-in-the-middle attacks** are a type of cyberattack where hackers set up rogue Wi-Fi hotspots in public places—often labeled as "Free_Wifi" or "Starbucks_Guest." Once connected, the attacker can intercept everything you send: login credentials, credit card numbers, personal emails, and even VPN traffic if it's not properly encrypted. This is especially dangerous for people who do mobile banking, file transfers, or online shopping while on-the-go.

Even **Bluetooth can be hijacked**. Attacks like BlueBorne and BlueSnarfing allow hackers to exploit Bluetooth connections to steal files, contacts, or even take control of your device—all without any interaction. Keeping Bluetooth turned on in crowded places like airports, conferences, or concerts increases your exposure significantly.

Your device is also a **gateway to social engineering attacks**. Phishing messages delivered via SMS (known as smishing) or messaging apps can look identical to legitimate sources. Clicking on a link in a fake delivery notice or bank message can install malware instantly or redirect you to a spoofed site that steals your login information. What makes this worse is that mobile users are more likely to skim, tap quickly, and fall victim due to the limited screen space and rushed pace.

To make matters more complex, **mobile operating systems are not foolproof.** While Apple's iOS and Android implement sandboxing, encryption, and regular updates, these security layers can be bypassed through jailbreaking, outdated software, or zero-day vulnerabilities that haven't been patched yet. Once compromised, your device becomes a surveillance tool—recording every keystroke, unlocking every password, and transmitting data without your knowledge.

In summary, mobile devices are treasure troves of data—making them high-value targets in the eyes of both malicious hackers and data-hungry corporations. The threats are real, constant, and evolving. But that doesn't mean you're defenseless. In the following chapters, we'll break down specific tools and techniques to protect yourself: from app permissions and encryption to secure messaging apps, mobile VPNs, and real-time threat detection.

For now, remember this: **If you wouldn't leave your wallet, passport, or diary lying around in public, don't do it digitally either.** Your smartphone is all three—and much more.

Carlos Mobile Cybercrime story

Carlos had just landed in New York after a business trip to Mexico City. As he made his way through JFK airport, he opened his phone to check emails, order an Uber, and notify his wife that he had landed. It was just another busy Monday—until it wasn't.

By the time he got into the Uber, Carlos noticed something strange. His bank app logged him out unexpectedly. Thinking it was just a glitch, he reopened it and typed in his password. Wrong. Then again. Wrong again. He stared at the screen in disbelief. He hadn't changed it. No one else knew it. And he had used it just a few hours ago to book his hotel.

Shrugging it off, he tried logging into his email instead—but was met with a message: "Your password has been changed. If this wasn't you, click here." A sinking feeling hit his stomach.

Within minutes, Carlos's phone began buzzing uncontrollably. His credit card company alerted him of a $1,500 transaction in Chicago. Then came a push notification that his Apple ID had been accessed from a different device. Then another for his Dropbox. He hadn't even left the airport, and his digital life was unraveling faster than he could react.

How had this happened?

Three days earlier, while enjoying a coffee at a quiet café in Mexico City, Carlos had connected to the café's free Wi-Fi. It was convenient, and he'd done it countless times in different cities. That morning, he had uploaded sensitive client documents to his Google Drive, logged into his investment account, and replied to several business emails. All over that free network.

What Carlos didn't realize was that the network wasn't really free—it was a fake hotspot set up by a hacker named Leo, sitting just two tables away. Leo's laptop was running packet-sniffing software, silently capturing login credentials, email headers, and session cookies from every device connected to the network.

But Leo wasn't done. The next step was a silent push of a fake system update to Carlos's Android phone through a technique known as a "man-in-the-middle" attack. Carlos tapped "Accept" without thinking, and unknowingly gave permission for malware to install in the background.

The malware was disguised as a routine update, but it embedded a keylogger and remote access tool (RAT). From that moment forward, Leo could see everything—every text Carlos typed, every password entered, even what his camera saw. And once Carlos connected to JFK's public Wi-Fi again, the malware woke back up and relayed the stored data straight to Leo's server.

Back at home, Carlos tried to fix the damage. He changed his passwords, called his bank, froze his credit, and reset his phone. But the damage had been done. Sensitive documents had been accessed. His identity was now part of the dark web. And the trust he once had in technology was shaken.

A week later, Carlos spoke with a cybersecurity expert. The expert walked him through every vulnerability in his routine: using public Wi-Fi without a VPN, not checking app permissions, leaving Bluetooth on in public spaces, and falling for fake system update messages. It was a brutal wake-up call.

But Carlos wasn't alone. Millions of people, every day, unknowingly walk into these traps. They click without reading. Connect without thinking. Install without verifying. And by the time they notice something's wrong, the attackers are already long gone—with data, photos, passwords, or worse.

Determined not to be a victim again, Carlos started to take mobile security seriously. He researched encrypted messaging apps, switched to a more secure cloud storage system, used a trusted VPN, and reviewed every app on his phone. He even learned how to recognize fake apps and phishing links. He made it a mission to protect not just himself, but also his wife and kids, by teaching them the same principles.

Carlos's story is not an anomaly—it's a modern cautionary tale. And it's exactly why this book exists. To help everyday people realize just how exposed we are in the mobile-first world, and how we can reclaim control through awareness, habit, and the right tools.

Chapter 2: Understanding App Permissions and How They Exploit You

Every time you install a new app, you're asked for permissions. Sometimes they're obvious: a navigation app needs location access; a camera app needs to use your camera. But what happens when a flashlight app asks for microphone access? Or when a photo editing app wants your contact list? The truth is, app permissions are one of the most overlooked yet exploited elements of mobile device security.

Permissions are the bridges between an app and your phone's internal functions. These include access to your location, microphone, camera, calendar, messages, photos, phone call history, biometric data, storage, and even your screen activity. Each permission, if misused, can become a gateway to surveillance or data theft. The problem is that most people simply click "Allow" without thinking—or worse, set apps to "Always Allow" when "Only While Using the App" would suffice.

Let's break down how these permissions are commonly abused. A seemingly harmless app could ask for location access and then quietly sell your movement data to advertisers or data brokers. Another might collect your clipboard history—meaning if you've copied passwords or credit card numbers, they're fair game. Some apps ask for SMS access under the guise of verification, but then use it to intercept two-factor authentication codes or spam your contacts.

Then there's **microphone and camera access**. An app that has access to both could technically record you or take pictures without your knowledge. Although mobile operating systems require apps to request these permissions explicitly, some malicious apps find ways to exploit loopholes—especially on outdated or jailbroken devices. Even legitimate apps have been caught recording user behavior in the background under the guise of "analytics."

Permissions can also change over time. You may install an app and approve a limited set of access privileges. But in a future update, the app might request additional permissions—and if you've enabled automatic updates, you may never realize the app has gained access to more of your personal data. This is called **permission creep**, and it's incredibly common.

So how do you take back control? Start by **reviewing every app's permissions manually**. On Android, go to Settings > Privacy > Permission Manager. On iOS, go to Settings > Privacy & Security, then tap each category (like Microphone or Camera) to see which apps have access. Revoke any permissions that don't make logical sense for the app's function.

You can also install **permission monitoring tools**. Apps like Bouncer (Android) allow you to grant temporary permissions that automatically expire after use. Other tools, like Jumbo or DuckDuckGo App Tracking Protection, block third-party trackers and provide visibility into how your data is being accessed and transmitted.

Next, **pay attention to how you install apps**. Always use official app stores (Google Play, Apple App Store), and avoid third-party APKs unless you trust the source. Before installing, check the developer name, app reviews, download count, and recent update history. Be wary of apps that are clones or have few reviews—these are often used as trojan horses for malware.

Even among legitimate apps, consider alternatives that request fewer permissions. For example, there are calculators that don't need internet access. Messaging apps like Signal are end-to-end encrypted and don't request access to your contacts unless you give it. Just because an app is popular doesn't mean it respects your privacy.

One more powerful step is using **mobile operating system features** that limit background access. Both iOS and Android allow you to restrict apps from refreshing in the background or using location services when not in use. These features can prevent apps from tracking or pinging your location every few minutes.

Ultimately, the best defense is **awareness combined with digital hygiene**. Make it a monthly habit to audit your phone—delete unused apps, check for unusual permission requests, and keep your OS and apps updated. The more you control what your apps can do, the less control third parties have over your life.

Understanding app permissions isn't just about tweaking settings—it's about protecting your data, your identity, and your peace of mind. The convenience of mobile technology should never come at the cost of silent surveillance.

How Ava learned the cost of privacy

Ava loved photography. As an aspiring content creator in her early twenties, she spent hours taking scenic shots with her iPhone and editing them with the latest trendy apps. On a weekend getaway to Arizona, she stumbled across a new app called *ProFilter+*. It promised Hollywood-level filters and pro editing features—for free. Without hesitation, she downloaded it, tapped "Allow" for every permission, and started exploring.

It wasn't until three days later that things started feeling... off.

Her battery drained unusually fast. She noticed her phone heating up even when she wasn't using it. One night, while messaging her sister, her screen froze, and a strange pop-up appeared—asking for access to her Bluetooth. She dismissed it, thinking it was a glitch, but a quiet sense of unease settled in.

That evening, while scrolling through TikTok, she saw a video about "spy apps" that secretly access your camera and microphone. Curious and a little spooked, Ava went into her phone settings and checked which apps had microphone access. To her surprise, *ProFilter+* was listed—not just for microphone and camera, but also for location, contacts, and even her motion sensors.

Why would a photo editing app need all of that?

She kept digging. Under *Settings > Privacy & Security*, she opened her Location Services. Again, *ProFilter+* was set to "Always Allow." She hadn't even realized. In the app's settings page, a note showed that the app had accessed her location 67 times in the past 24 hours. Her stomach dropped.

Worse, the app had a permission to access her contacts. That explained the strange email her friend Lena had received from an unfamiliar address linked to Ava's name. It read like spam—cryptic links and random emojis. Lena had replied asking if she was hacked. At the time, Ava brushed it off as phishing. Now she wasn't so sure.

Feeling exposed, Ava deleted *ProFilter+* immediately. But she needed answers. She called a tech-savvy friend, Malik, who worked in cybersecurity. After hearing her story, he agreed to help. Malik asked Ava to install a privacy auditing app, which instantly flagged *ProFilter+* as a risk. It had been running in the background constantly, transmitting metadata and sensor data to a remote server in Eastern Europe.

"Even though you deleted it," Malik explained, "it likely collected weeks of behavioral patterns, GPS logs, and even access to your microphone. Some of these apps activate your mic during 'quiet' hours just to profile ambient sound or collect voice samples. Not all of them need to record to monetize."

Ava was shocked. "But it was on the App Store," she said.

"Doesn't mean it's safe," Malik replied. "Sometimes these apps pass the review process but update their behavior afterward. Plus, many users never check permissions. Developers count on that."

Together, they spent the next hour scrubbing her phone—revoking excessive permissions, turning off background app refresh, disabling location for all but essential apps, and installing a reliable VPN and privacy firewall. They also found five other apps that requested camera or microphone access unnecessarily—games, shopping apps, even a horoscope app she hadn't used in months.

The biggest revelation? Ava realized she had never questioned why apps needed what they asked for. It had always been automatic: tap "Install," tap "Allow," and move on.

From that day on, Ava changed how she approached her phone. She now audited her permissions monthly. Before installing anything new, she researched the developer, read privacy policies, and double-checked what access it needed. She also found alternative apps that didn't require invasive permissions.

Her phone felt lighter, faster, and safer. She no longer felt like she was being watched. More importantly, she regained a sense of control.

The next time a new editing app went viral, Ava paused. She opened the listing, scrolled through the permissions, and asked herself: "Does it really need access to all this?"

Most people don't realize how much they're giving away with a single tap. But Ava had learned the hard way that convenience can come at the cost of privacy—and she wasn't going to make that mistake again.

Chapter 3: Public Wi-Fi, Bluetooth, and Location Tracking Risks

In an always-connected world, mobile convenience comes at a cost. Public Wi-Fi networks, Bluetooth signals, and location tracking services are all features designed to make life easier—but they also create major vulnerabilities that can be exploited without you ever realizing it. The challenge lies in understanding how these tools work and how they can be manipulated by attackers, advertisers, and even the apps you trust.

Let's start with **public Wi-Fi**, one of the most common and dangerous mobile security threats. Cafés, airports, hotels, and even shopping malls offer free Wi-Fi as a perk—but "free" often comes with hidden costs. These networks are frequently unsecured, meaning they don't use encryption to protect the data you send or receive. Any information you transmit over HTTP sites—emails, passwords, credit card numbers—can be intercepted using basic tools like packet sniffers or Wireshark. Worse, hackers can set up **rogue hotspots**—networks named "Free_WiFi" or "Starbucks_Guest"—that look legitimate but are actually controlled by attackers. Once connected, they can launch man-in-the-middle attacks, intercept data, inject malware, or impersonate trusted websites.

Even encrypted HTTPS traffic isn't completely immune if attackers can trick users into installing a fake certificate authority or exploit a vulnerability in the device's browser. Mobile banking, file syncing, or even signing into a cloud account over public Wi-Fi can open the door to massive data loss if done without protection.

The second major risk factor is **Bluetooth**. Most people leave Bluetooth enabled by default for convenience—syncing with headphones, cars, or smartwatches. But Bluetooth operates as a constant, low-energy signal broadcaster. It can be discovered and connected to by other devices within a short range, typically 10 to 30 feet. Vulnerabilities like BlueBorne, discovered in 2017, showed that attackers could connect to and control a device simply by being nearby—even without the user accepting a pairing request. Other attacks like Bluesnarfing can allow data extraction or unauthorized access to the device file system.

Turning off Bluetooth when not actively using it is a basic but powerful defense. Even if you trust your headphones, you don't need Bluetooth active 24/7, especially in public places like airports, conferences, or public transit systems. Bluetooth also drains your battery, so disabling it can help with both security and performance.

The third critical but often misunderstood vector is **location tracking**. Most smartphones use a combination of GPS, Wi-Fi triangulation, and cell tower signals to determine your precise location. This feature powers useful tools—like maps, weather alerts, rideshare apps, and emergency response. But it's also a privacy minefield.

Apps that collect location data often share or sell it to third-party advertisers and data brokers. Some apps track your movement continuously—even when not in use—and store it indefinitely. This data can be aggregated to create a detailed profile of your daily habits: where you work, shop, sleep, and travel. Worse, this information can be subpoenaed, hacked, or sold to marketers who then serve targeted ads—or, in extreme cases, leaked to the public.

To take control, begin by auditing location permissions on your device. Only allow access "While Using the App" unless absolutely necessary. Turn off "Precise Location" if it's not required. Disable "Background App Refresh" for apps that don't need to constantly update. You can also toggle off "Significant Locations" on iPhones or "Google Location History" on Android to stop your device from tracking your every move.

Another tool to consider is a **mobile VPN**, which encrypts your internet connection—especially useful when accessing public Wi-Fi. VPNs mask your IP address, prevent ISPs and hackers from seeing your browsing activity, and create an encrypted tunnel for your data. Choose a reputable, paid VPN with a no-logs policy. Free VPNs often come with tradeoffs like selling your data or injecting ads.

Finally, turn off **automatic connection settings** that allow your phone to connect to open Wi-Fi networks without asking. This setting is often enabled by default and can cause your phone to reconnect to malicious hotspots you've encountered in the past.

In summary, your phone's ability to connect wirelessly to networks, devices, and satellites is a double-edged sword. These features enable convenience, speed, and functionality—but also expose you to real-time threats if left unchecked. By becoming intentional about how you use Wi-Fi, Bluetooth, and location services, you can dramatically reduce your digital footprint and limit exposure to unauthorized access or data harvesting.

The goal isn't to fear these features—it's to use them wisely. In the next chapter, we'll explore how to set up your smartphone for **maximum security**, including encrypted messaging apps, secure storage options, and the best privacy settings on both iOS and Android.

Now, let's go over Jordan's banking app story

Jordan was a digital nomad—a freelance designer who spent his time working from cafés in Bali, co-working spaces in Lisbon, and airport lounges across the world. His phone was his life. It held client contracts, design drafts, banking apps, passwords, and the video calls he used to close deals. But for all his tech-savviness, Jordan was careless in one area: convenience.

On a rainy Tuesday in Chiang Mai, Thailand, Jordan sat at a cozy café, sipping an espresso and reviewing a $12,000 client contract. He connected to the café's free Wi-Fi, uploaded some design files, and checked his banking app. Nothing seemed unusual.

That night, while lying in bed at his Airbnb, his phone buzzed with a banking notification. A transaction for $3,900 had just been authorized on his debit card in Singapore. His heart skipped. He hadn't been to Singapore in months. A second alert followed. Then a third.

Panic set in. He opened his banking app—it required a two-factor authentication code, but the message never arrived.

He checked his inbox. No reset email. Something was very wrong.

Jordan jumped on a secure laptop and contacted his bank's fraud team. After a tense 20-minute call, he learned that his account had been accessed by someone using a near-identical device ID from a Southeast Asian IP address. They had logged in, reset his email password, and redirected his SMS verification codes using a spoofing technique. Jordan had been hacked—and he had no idea how.

The next morning, he visited a local cybersecurity expert. After a quick inspection, they found the root of the problem: Jordan had connected to a rogue Wi-Fi network. It mimicked the café's legitimate one but had a slightly different name: "TheBean_Cafe_Free" instead of "Bean_Cafe_Free." The attacker had used a man-in-the-middle attack to intercept his traffic, inject a fake banking site, and steal his credentials in real time.

Even worse, Jordan had left **Bluetooth on**. The hacker used a technique called BlueSnarfing to extract files from his phone and remotely installed a malicious script using a Bluetooth exploit. His contacts, notes, and location history were all exposed.

To top it off, the expert showed him that his phone's **location tracking** was active—and his movements had been logged for weeks. "Look," the expert said, pointing at a timeline on the screen. "It knows exactly where you were on March 2nd at 9:13 a.m.—down to the café seat you sat in."

Jordan stared, speechless. His entire life had been mapped, compromised, and monetized. All without him knowing.

It wasn't that he was ignorant. He had simply trusted convenience. The expert guided him through a series of fixes: revoking app permissions, disabling Bluetooth auto-connect, clearing saved Wi-Fi networks, turning off precise location, and installing a premium VPN with real-time protection. Jordan also enabled "Ask to Join Networks" so he'd never auto-connect again.

The next few days felt different. He was cautious. He avoided public Wi-Fi unless using a VPN. He turned Bluetooth off when not in use. He began manually reviewing every permission request from his apps and disabled GPS tracking except for maps and ride-sharing.

Jordan's story became a lesson he shared with every freelancer he met. Over time, he even created a short guide called "Freelancer Cyber Hygiene 101," which he shared for free on his website. The same guy who once brushed off digital security was now warning others that their mobile freedom had a price—and that price was their data.

He'd learned the hard way that **connectivity without caution is like leaving your front door wide open in a busy city.**

Security didn't mean locking down everything—it meant being smart about what you allowed and when.

Chapter 4: Securing Your Smartphone — Settings, Tools, and Best Practices

Securing your smartphone begins with a shift in mindset: your phone is not just a device—it's your identity, your wallet, and your private life all wrapped into a single object that you carry everywhere. Every tap, download, or swipe opens a new opportunity—either for productivity or for exploitation. Fortunately, modern smartphones come with powerful built-in protections—you just have to use them properly. This chapter provides a step-by-step guide to locking down your phone using smart settings, free tools, and proven habits.

First, let's start with your **lock screen**. It's your first line of defense. Use a strong, six-digit PIN or alphanumeric passcode instead of a simple four-digit code. Biometric authentication—such as Face ID or fingerprint—is convenient, but should always be paired with a strong backup code. Never use swipe patterns or facial unlocks that rely only on front-facing cameras—they can be bypassed with photos or smudges. Also, disable lock screen previews for sensitive apps like email, texts, or banking to prevent prying eyes from seeing notifications without unlocking your phone.

Next, check for and enable **automatic security updates**. Both Android and iOS release critical security patches regularly. Enable "Auto-Install Updates" to make sure your apps and OS are always up to date. An unpatched phone is the most vulnerable kind of device, especially with the increasing discovery of zero-day exploits.

One of the most overlooked settings is **App Permissions Review**. Every month, review which apps have access to your camera, microphone, contacts, calendar, and location. Ask yourself: does this app really need this level of access to function? If not, revoke it. On Android, go to Settings > Privacy > Permission Manager. On iOS, go to Settings > Privacy & Security. Revoke permissions from any app that doesn't need it, or switch to "Only While Using App" for those that do.

To protect data at rest, **encrypt your phone storage**. Most iPhones do this by default. On Android, go to Settings > Security > Encryption. If your phone allows it, turn on full-disk encryption. This ensures that even if your phone is stolen, the contents cannot be accessed without the decryption key (your passcode).

Another essential habit is **regular backups**. Use encrypted cloud backups or local encrypted backups through iTunes (iOS) or ADB (Android). Avoid third-party backup apps that ask for excessive permissions or send data to unknown servers.

In the event of theft, damage, or malware, a backup is your recovery lifeline.

Now let's talk about **secure messaging**. Avoid default SMS for any sensitive communication. Instead, use end-to-end encrypted apps like Signal, WhatsApp, or Telegram (with secret chats enabled). Signal is the most privacy-respecting option, as it doesn't store metadata or message logs. Enable disappearing messages and biometric lock features within these apps to add an extra layer of protection.

Install a **trusted VPN** on your phone—especially if you regularly connect to public Wi-Fi. A VPN encrypts your internet traffic, making it unreadable to hackers or ISPs. Reputable providers include ProtonVPN, Mullvad, NordVPN, and ExpressVPN. Never use free VPNs unless they have a proven no-logs policy and good reviews, as many sell your data or inject ads.

For Android users, consider installing **privacy firewalls** like NetGuard or TrackerControl. These tools allow you to see which apps are making internet connections, block suspicious behavior, and stop background data leaks. iOS users can benefit from apps like Lockdown Privacy or Guardian Firewall.

Next, disable **ad tracking and analytics sharing**. On iOS, go to Settings > Privacy & Security > Tracking, and turn off

"Allow Apps to Request to Track." On Android, go to Settings > Google > Ads, and enable "Opt out of Ads Personalization." You should also reset your device's advertising ID regularly.

For additional safety, turn off features like **AirDrop**, **NFC**, and **Nearby Share** when not in use. These are convenient tools, but they also allow unknown devices to send you files or requests. Bluetooth and Wi-Fi should be disabled when not in use, especially in public areas.

Finally, enable **Find My Device** or **Find My iPhone**, which lets you remotely locate, lock, or wipe your phone if lost or stolen. This should be set up immediately upon purchasing a new device. On iPhones, it's part of iCloud. On Android, you can find it under Google > Find My Device.

These settings and practices may take 30 minutes to configure, but they will protect you from years of potential breaches, stress, and financial loss. Your phone will run smoother, leak less data, and give you peace of mind knowing you're no longer easy prey.

In the next chapter, we'll explore **how to protect your personal communications and files**, including encrypted cloud storage, secure calling, and privacy-first alternatives to common apps.

Now, let's talk about Riley's story

Riley had always assumed her iPhone was secure. It was sleek, expensive, and always updated. She never clicked on suspicious links, and she kept her apps to a minimum. But one evening, after attending a cybersecurity seminar at her local university, she realized how much she'd taken for granted.

The speaker, a retired ethical hacker named Sam, demonstrated how easy it was to exploit a phone with just a few overlooked settings. He mirrored his screen and showed how, in less than ten minutes, he had remotely accessed a test device—thanks to weak lock screen settings and an old app that hadn't been updated in over a year. The room was silent.

Riley went home that night with a pit in her stomach. She picked up her phone and began to think differently—not as a tool, but as a potential open door.

She opened her settings. The first thing she changed was her passcode. She had been using the same four-digit code since college. It was easy to remember—but even easier to guess. She replaced it with a twelve-character alphanumeric passphrase, something strong but meaningful to her.

Next, she dove into app permissions. It stunned her to see that a random game she hadn't used in six months still had access to her camera and microphone. Why would it need that? She revoked its access immediately. Then came her calendar, contacts, and location. She found apps she didn't even remember installing still tracking her movements. One app had requested "Always" location access and had quietly logged every place she visited for months.

Feeling unnerved, she turned to her messaging apps. Her default app was still SMS—completely unencrypted. She downloaded Signal, set it as her primary messenger, and imported her contacts. It was a small change, but it gave her comfort knowing her conversations wouldn't be stored on a cloud server or intercepted mid-transmission.

Then she addressed Wi-Fi. She had dozens of networks saved—cafés, hotels, even an old network from her ex's house. She wiped them all, then disabled "Auto-Join" for public networks. From now on, if she needed to use free Wi-Fi, it would be behind a VPN. She subscribed to ProtonVPN and set it to launch automatically on public networks.

Bluetooth? Off when not in use. Background app refresh? Disabled for all but essential apps. Ad tracking? Turned off. Her "Significant Locations" feature? Disabled. It had been recording visits to her therapist's office, her friend's houses, and her favorite park. The digital breadcrumb trail stunned her.

Finally, she enabled "Find My iPhone" and double-checked her iCloud settings. She set her backups to encrypt automatically and made a note to back up her phone weekly. For good measure, she downloaded a mobile firewall app to monitor outbound data connections—something she never even knew existed before the seminar.

The next morning, Riley's phone felt different. It wasn't just faster—it felt lighter, more private, more hers. She hadn't realized how many open doors she had left unguarded.

Two weeks later, her friend Dana messaged her in a panic. Her email had been hacked, and her phone was acting strangely. Riley didn't just sympathize—she helped. She walked Dana through the same settings she had secured. Together, they turned a scary moment into a valuable lesson.

What started as a quiet concern turned into empowerment. Riley wasn't an expert, but she no longer felt helpless. She had transformed her phone from a risk into a fortress—one tap, one setting, one decision at a time.

And she made a new rule for herself: every month, she would audit her digital life—just like she did with her finances and health. Because protecting your phone isn't just about tech—it's about peace of mind.

Chapter 5: Protecting Personal Files, Photos, and Cloud Data

Your smartphone is more than a communication device—it's a personal vault. It stores thousands of photos, private documents, scanned IDs, contracts, financial records, and even sensitive notes. While smartphones are incredibly convenient for managing your life, that same convenience makes them high-value targets for theft, hacking, and surveillance. If your files, photos, or cloud storage accounts are compromised, the impact can be devastating—from identity theft and extortion to financial loss and emotional stress.

The first step in protecting your personal data is to understand how it's stored and shared. Most mobile users rely heavily on **cloud services** like iCloud, Google Drive, OneDrive, or Dropbox to store and back up files. These services are efficient, but they're not immune to attacks or data leaks. A data breach of your cloud account can give attackers access to your entire digital life, especially if you reuse passwords or don't use two-factor authentication.

Start by **securing your cloud accounts with strong, unique passwords** and enabling **two-factor authentication (2FA)**. Avoid using SMS-based 2FA if possible, as it can be intercepted through SIM swapping.

Instead, use an authentication app like Authy, Google Authenticator, or Microsoft Authenticator. For even more control, consider using a hardware security key like YubiKey.

Next, review **sharing permissions** on cloud-stored files. It's common to forget that a document you shared with someone last year might still be accessible to others via a public or semi-private link. Go into your cloud storage settings and audit shared files and folders. Revoke access to anything that no longer needs to be available to others, and avoid using "Anyone with the link can view" settings unless absolutely necessary.

Encrypt sensitive files before uploading them to the cloud. You can use tools like **Cryptomator** (for both Android and iOS), **VeraCrypt**, or **7-Zip** to encrypt files with a password before storing them online. This way, even if your cloud storage account is breached, the encrypted files remain unreadable without the decryption key.

On your phone, use **secure file vault apps** to store private photos, PDFs, and notes. Many apps provide encrypted, password-protected containers that are not accessible from the general file browser or photo gallery. Examples include **Keepsafe**, **Folder Lock**, or **Proton Drive**. Ensure these apps are regularly updated and use biometric locks in addition to strong passwords.

For photo protection, disable automatic syncing for sensitive folders unless you trust the cloud provider's security. If you use Google Photos or iCloud, review what folders are being backed up. Consider setting up a separate private vault for ID photos, receipts, and anything else you wouldn't want leaked or accessed without permission.

Also be cautious with **scanner apps**. These tools are often used to digitize passports, licenses, or tax documents—but many scanner apps store files in cloud servers by default. Choose apps that offer local-only storage, end-to-end encryption, and clear privacy policies. **Adobe Scan**, **Scanbot**, and **Genius Scan+** are among the more privacy-conscious options.

Regularly back up your files **offline** using an encrypted external drive or SD card, and store that backup in a secure place. Cloud storage is convenient but not foolproof—files can be deleted, corrupted, or locked in a ransomware attack. A local, offline backup acts as your last line of defense.

Finally, pay close attention to **app permissions and file access**. Some apps, especially photo editors, social media platforms, or file managers, request full access to your photo gallery, camera roll, and file system. Ask yourself whether the app truly needs that access—or whether a privacy-respecting alternative exists.

As an added layer of defense, you can install mobile security suites with **data leak detection** and **anti-theft features**. Tools like **Bitdefender Mobile Security**, **Avast Mobile Security**, or **Lookout** can alert you when your data appears in known breaches, and allow remote wiping of files if your device is lost or stolen.

In the end, protecting your personal files and photos comes down to one principle: **if it's valuable to you, it's valuable to someone else.** Treat every photo, document, and scan with the same care you would give to your wallet or passport. Encrypt it, lock it, and know where it's stored—and you'll be far ahead of most mobile users who unknowingly leave their lives wide open to the world.

In the next chapter, we'll take a deep dive into **safe mobile messaging, calling, and video chats**, including the best encrypted communication apps and how to stop your conversations from being monitored, recorded, or leaked.

Natasha's strange email story

Natasha was a successful freelance attorney who ran her practice entirely from her phone and laptop. Contracts, case notes, sensitive client files—everything was stored in neatly organized folders on her Google Drive. Her iPhone synced automatically to iCloud, and she used Dropbox to back up her scanned documents and ID photos.

But one day, that digital organization turned into a liability.

She was in the middle of onboarding a new corporate client when she received a strange email. It appeared to be from Google, warning that someone had tried to access her Drive from a device in Russia. At first, she assumed it was a phishing scam—until she checked her login activity. There it was: a real login from Moscow. Someone had gotten in.

Panicking, Natasha changed her password and logged out of all devices. But the damage had been done. Two confidential legal contracts and a folder labeled "Clients_2024" had been downloaded. That same day, she received an anonymous email with a screenshot of one of those files—and a demand for $5,000 in crypto or the information would be leaked.

She sat frozen, heart racing. Her entire reputation, years of trust with clients, could be shattered.

After recovering her composure, Natasha contacted a cybersecurity specialist. Together, they investigated the breach. It turned out that Natasha had reused a slightly modified version of the same password across her Dropbox, Google, and iCloud accounts. One of those passwords had already been leaked in a past data breach, and without two-factor authentication enabled, her Google Drive became an easy target.

The specialist explained something that would stick with her forever: "Your cloud account is not private unless you make it private. And your phone is only as secure as your weakest password."

They immediately set up a security overhaul. She enabled two-factor authentication on every cloud service using a physical security key. Then, they downloaded Cryptomator and encrypted her most sensitive folders before uploading them. Now, even if her account was compromised, the files would be unreadable without the decryption key stored locally.

She also stopped using scanner apps that automatically synced to Dropbox. Instead, she used Genius Scan+ with local storage, and only uploaded files manually to an encrypted folder. The automatic syncing had made her life easy—but had also meant that every scanned passport, license, and signed document was floating in the cloud.

Natasha's photo gallery was another eye-opener. She had over 5,000 pictures, including personal selfies, client IDs, screenshots of wire transfers, and photos of handwritten notes. She disabled photo backups for sensitive albums, deleted hundreds of images, and installed a private photo vault with biometric locking. "This isn't about paranoia," she told herself. "It's about professionalism."

By the time they finished, Natasha had a local encrypted backup on an external drive, encrypted cloud storage with two-factor protection, and app-specific passwords for each device. She had gone from exposed to empowered in just a few days.

A week later, she gave a short seminar to a group of women entrepreneurs. She walked them through everything she'd learned: how to encrypt cloud files, how to use privacy-first scanner apps, and why storing copies of your passport on your phone is risky without a secure vault.

Natasha wasn't a tech expert. But she was now more secure than 95% of smartphone users.

Her takeaway? “Don’t wait for a breach to take action. If it’s important enough to store, it’s important enough to protect.”

Chapter 6: Safe Messaging, Calling, and Video Chats on Mobile

Texting, voice calls, and video chats are the most frequent ways people communicate through their smartphones. But what many users don't realize is that these conversations are not always private. From insecure default messaging apps to unencrypted video platforms and data-logging telecom providers, your mobile communications are more exposed than you think. In an era of surveillance capitalism and digital eavesdropping, securing your conversations is not a luxury—it's a necessity.

Let's begin with **text messaging (SMS)**. SMS is one of the least secure communication methods available. Messages are transmitted in plain text and can be intercepted by telecom providers, law enforcement, or attackers using signal interception technology. In many countries, SMS logs—including message content, time, and recipient—are stored by the carrier for months or even years. If you care about privacy, using SMS should be limited to non-sensitive conversations only.

Instead, switch to **end-to-end encrypted messaging apps**, where only the sender and recipient can read the messages—even the service provider can't decrypt them. The top choices include:

- **Signal**: Widely considered the most secure messaging app. It's open-source, has no ads, doesn't collect metadata, and offers disappearing messages, screen security, and encrypted voice/video calls.
- **WhatsApp**: Owned by Meta, WhatsApp uses end-to-end encryption for messages and calls, but it collects metadata like who you contact and when.
- **Telegram**: Offers end-to-end encryption in Secret Chats only (not by default). Its cloud-based chat system is fast but less private if you don't enable secure mode.
- **Threema** and **Wire**: Less popular but extremely secure and privacy-focused. Great for professionals and enterprises.

Next, consider **voice and video calls**. Your default phone app is likely routed through your carrier's VoLTE or GSM network, which is not encrypted end-to-end. Conversations can be logged or intercepted using SS7 protocol vulnerabilities. For private calls, use apps like **Signal**, **WhatsApp**, or **FaceTime** (for iOS users), all of which use end-to-end encryption for voice and video.

Be careful with **recording permissions**. Many video conferencing and messaging apps request access to your microphone and camera—even when not in use. Always check in your settings whether an app is accessing your mic or cam in the background. Both iOS and Android now alert users when the mic or camera is active, usually with a colored dot or icon in the corner of the screen.

Limit microphone access to trusted apps only, and disable it completely for any app that doesn't need it. On Android, go to Settings > Privacy > Permission Manager > Microphone. On iOS, go to Settings > Privacy & Security > Microphone.

When using **video conferencing apps** like Zoom, Google Meet, or Microsoft Teams, be aware that not all of them are fully encrypted. Some platforms offer encryption only for paid users, and others log metadata extensively. If you're handling sensitive business conversations or legal discussions, opt for secure options like Signal or Jitsi Meet (open-source and free).

For additional protection, consider using **voice masking, burner phone numbers**, or anonymous messaging when dealing with high-risk situations. Apps like **Burner** or **Hushed** let you create temporary phone numbers for calls and texts, which can be used without exposing your real number.

Also, beware of **social engineering via messaging platforms**. Attackers can impersonate a trusted contact and trick you into clicking malicious links, downloading spyware, or sharing sensitive information. Always verify the identity of someone sending urgent requests, especially if they're asking for money, login credentials, or private files.

To further lock down your communications, use features like **two-factor authentication** on all messaging apps, **PIN codes** for chat access, and **disappearing messages** that auto-delete after a set time. Many apps now allow you to protect specific conversations with biometric locks or secondary passwords.

Lastly, audit your message backups. Some apps, like WhatsApp, back up messages to Google Drive or iCloud—these backups are often **not encrypted**, even if the messages themselves are. Disable cloud backups or enable encrypted backups if your app supports it.

In summary, secure communication requires more than choosing the right app. It's a combination of encrypted tools, awareness of permissions, strong account protection, and smart habits. Whether you're chatting with friends, conducting business, or sharing personal updates, every message you send can either remain private—or become someone else's opportunity.

In the next chapter, we'll dive into **mobile app traps and spyware threats**, exploring how legitimate-looking apps and hidden stalkerware can turn your phone into a surveillance device.

How Lena learned the importance of encryption

Lena worked in investigative journalism. Her work focused on exposing corruption in business and government, often dealing with confidential sources and whistleblowers. While she took her reporting seriously, she hadn't fully considered just how insecure her mobile communication habits had become.

She texted sources using regular SMS, made calls using her carrier's default app, and used video chat to conduct interviews. One day, while covering a corporate cover-up story, she received a tip from a source who warned her, "Be careful. They might be monitoring you."

At first, she brushed it off. She wasn't hacking into servers—just reporting facts. But that same night, she noticed her phone acting strangely. Her camera light flickered briefly, even though she wasn't using it. Her phone heated up for no reason, and a call she made to her editor dropped after just a few seconds. Something wasn't right.

The next day, she met with a digital security expert from a nonprofit press freedom organization. After a few simple checks, the expert's expression turned serious.

"Your texts and calls aren't encrypted. You're using the default apps. And your phone's microphone has been accessed by a third-party app recently—without your knowledge."

Lena's stomach dropped.

The expert explained that even though she thought she was being careful, her mobile habits were wide open. SMS messages, for example, can be intercepted through cell tower spoofing or even internal carrier access. And regular phone calls? Completely unencrypted. Her conversations—some with vulnerable sources—could have been monitored or recorded.

They began securing her phone immediately.

First, they installed **Signal**, a secure messaging app with end-to-end encryption for texts, voice, and video. The app required no backups, didn't store contact metadata, and allowed for timed disappearing messages. Then they configured **two-factor authentication** using a separate app—not SMS—and added a PIN to lock Signal access even if someone got into her phone.

Next, they disabled microphone access for every app that didn't need it. Lena was shocked to find that her workout app and photo editor both had microphone permissions. Why? She had no idea. The expert removed them all and turned on a feature that alerted her when the microphone or camera was in use.

They switched her cloud backups off for WhatsApp, which she had used occasionally with friends. She learned that, although WhatsApp encrypted messages, the backups to iCloud or Google Drive were **not encrypted** by default—making them a major risk if her cloud account was ever compromised.

For high-risk conversations, the expert recommended she use **burner phone numbers** with an app like Hushed, giving her the ability to communicate with sources without revealing her actual number. They also set her default calling method to Signal, so even her voice calls would be encrypted.

Later that week, Lena received another tip—this time from a new contact overseas. She was ready. The chat took place over Signal, with disappearing messages enabled. She took handwritten notes instead of recording the call, and nothing was backed up to the cloud.

A few months later, Lena published her investigation. The report made headlines. Behind the scenes, her sources remained safe, her phone remained clean, and no one could prove how she got the information.

She had learned a crucial lesson: being a professional in a digital world means **protecting not just your data, but your conversations**.

Lena now teaches mobile communication privacy to other journalists. She shares how your phone calls, texts, and video chats can be either private or permanent—and the choice is yours.

Chapter 7: Mobile App Traps, Malware, and Spyware Threats

Not all mobile apps are what they appear to be. Some pose as useful tools, games, or entertainment platforms—but behind the scenes, they collect your data, install tracking software, or even function as spyware. The modern smartphone has become a goldmine for developers and attackers alike, and mobile users who fail to recognize app-based traps leave themselves vulnerable to surveillance, identity theft, or worse. In this chapter, we'll expose the most common app-based threats and how to protect yourself from hidden dangers lurking in your downloads.

Let's begin with **malicious apps**. These are applications that look legitimate but are designed to steal data, install malware, or hijack device functions. They are most commonly found on third-party app stores or sketchy websites offering APK (Android app) files. However, some have even made it into official app stores like Google Play or the Apple App Store, often disguised as flashlight tools, wallpapers, QR code scanners, or utility apps. Once installed, they request excessive permissions and begin sending data to remote servers or monitoring your behavior.

One of the most dangerous types of mobile threats is **spyware**, also known as stalkerware. These are apps designed to silently track your device's location, text messages, call history, photos, and even microphone and camera activity—without your knowledge. Spyware can be installed by someone with temporary access to your device (such as a partner, employer, or stranger) and often runs in the background, hidden from the home screen or app drawer.

Spyware apps can appear as innocuous system updates or use generic names like "Device Helper" or "System Services" to avoid detection. Some are sold openly as "parental control" or "employee monitoring" tools but are often used for abuse or harassment. Once active, they transmit private data continuously and can even allow remote activation of your microphone or screen.

To protect against these threats, begin by **reviewing your installed apps** regularly. If you find apps you don't remember downloading or that request suspicious permissions, remove them immediately. On Android, go to Settings > Apps > See All Apps, and sort by most recently installed. On iPhone, navigate to Settings > General > iPhone Storage. Also check for "Device Admin" privileges under Settings > Security on Android—some spyware apps gain elevated permissions by masquerading as system tools.

Next, **install anti-malware or mobile security apps** from reputable companies such as Bitdefender, Malwarebytes, Norton, or Avast. These tools can scan your phone for hidden spyware, malicious code, and unauthorized app behavior. Some even monitor your microphone and camera usage for signs of surveillance.

Always download apps **only from trusted sources**. Avoid third-party app stores or sideloading apps from links in emails, text messages, or pop-up ads. Before downloading, review the developer name, app permissions, reviews, and download count. Be skeptical of apps with overly generic descriptions, excessive permissions, or sudden spikes in reviews that feel fake or repetitive.

Take special caution with **free apps** that ask for access to contacts, storage, call logs, or device history. Many of these apps earn revenue not by charging users, but by selling your data to third-party ad networks or data brokers. If a flashlight app needs to access your microphone and camera, something is wrong.

You should also disable the setting that allows **installation of unknown apps**. On Android, go to Settings > Apps > Special Access > Install Unknown Apps, and disable this feature for every app. On iPhone, although sideloading is more restricted, you should still avoid installing enterprise-signed apps unless absolutely necessary.

Another step to take is to **monitor your device's behavior**. If your battery drains quickly, the phone overheats, the screen stays on, or your mobile data usage spikes unexpectedly, those could be signs of background activity from malware or spyware. Also be alert to strange noises during phone calls, pop-ups, or changes in screen brightness.

If you suspect your phone is compromised, the safest solution is to **back up your files securely, perform a full factory reset**, and reinstall apps one by one—only from trusted sources. Avoid restoring full app data from cloud backups if spyware may be included in the backup files.

Finally, educate the people around you. Children, partners, and elderly relatives often download apps without reviewing permissions. Help them set up devices with app review settings, biometric access controls, and parental controls that aren't exploitable.

In a world where millions of apps are available with just a tap, your defense must be vigilance. Every app you install is either protecting your privacy—or silently draining it. The goal is not to avoid apps altogether, but to choose wisely, monitor behavior, and never give blanket trust to any program without earning it.

In the next chapter, we'll shift focus to **physical security**, discussing what to do if your phone is lost, stolen, or seized—and how to prevent unauthorized access in high-risk situations.

Now, let's go over Tasha's story

Tasha was a high school math teacher by day and a true-crime podcast junkie by night. She loved using her phone to organize lesson plans, message friends, and unwind with games after grading papers. One day, while scrolling through social media, she saw an ad for a productivity app that promised to help her track grades, create class schedules, and manage parent-teacher meetings all in one place. The app looked sleek, had hundreds of five-star reviews, and best of all—it was free.

She downloaded it without a second thought.

For the first week, everything seemed fine. The app worked well and even sent her reminders she found helpful. But soon, strange things started happening.

Tasha's phone would randomly buzz, even when she had no notifications. Her battery began draining twice as fast. She started getting ads for things she had only discussed out loud with her husband—never searched, never typed. One day, while walking into class, her phone restarted itself and displayed an error she'd never seen before.

Concerned, she mentioned it to a friend who worked in IT. He offered to take a quick look and ran a security scan on her phone. What he found shocked them both.

The app she had installed was flagged as spyware. Though it appeared legitimate, it was quietly uploading her contacts, microphone activity, location data, and even the contents of her clipboard—every time she copied a password or a note. Worse, it had been granted admin privileges, which meant it had deeper control over her phone than even she did. It was designed to be invisible and nearly impossible to remove without a full factory reset.

"I just thought it was a school planner," she whispered, realizing how much of her private life had been accessed and possibly sold.

Her friend explained that many malicious apps pass through app store filters using fake reviews and obfuscated code. Once installed, they harvest information silently, blend into system processes, and start feeding data to third-party servers or individuals who sell it for advertising—or more sinister purposes.

Together, they removed the app and performed a complete factory reset. He helped her install security software and taught her how to audit app permissions, check for device administrator access, and monitor background data activity. He showed her how to spot red flags: generic developer names, excessive permissions, and glowing reviews posted all on the same day.

That weekend, Tasha did a full audit of her apps. She was shocked to find a random QR code scanner that had access to her photos, a "notes" app that had microphone permission, and a flashlight app that was requesting location access. She deleted all of them.

She realized that convenience had made her careless. She had allowed unknown apps into her most personal space—her phone—and paid the price in lost privacy.

A month later, she gave a short presentation to the PTA on digital safety for families. Parents listened wide-eyed as she explained how kids unknowingly install spyware-laced games, and how even adults fall for the slickest-looking productivity apps. She shared her checklist for evaluating apps and emphasized the importance of saying "no" to unnecessary permissions.

From then on, she treated her phone the way she treated her classroom: only trusted people and tools allowed in—and everything monitored with intention.

Tasha's experience became a reminder that the biggest threats to mobile security often come dressed as helpful tools. And that sometimes, the scariest villains don't knock—they sneak in through the app store.

Chapter 8: What to Do If Your Phone Is Lost, Stolen, or Seized

Losing your phone is no longer just an inconvenience—it can be a full-blown digital emergency. Whether your device is misplaced, stolen by a thief, or seized by an authority, your private life could be exposed in minutes if the right protections aren't in place. Your contacts, bank apps, photos, messages, social media accounts, documents, and stored passwords are all potentially accessible. But with the right preparation, response, and settings, you can minimize the damage—or prevent it entirely.

Step 1: Prepare Before It Happens

The best time to defend your data is before your phone is lost or taken. Begin by enabling your device's **remote tracking and wipe features**:

- For iPhone users, go to Settings > [Your Name] > Find My > Find My iPhone, and enable both "Find My iPhone" and "Send Last Location."
- For Android users, go to Settings > Security > Find My Device (or use the Google Find My Device app). Enable both location tracking and remote erase options.

These tools allow you to locate your phone on a map, lock it remotely, and erase it if recovery isn't possible.

Second, ensure that your **lock screen is truly secure**. Use a complex passcode (not just 4 digits), and disable lock screen previews for sensitive notifications such as texts, emails, or messages. Remove access to Wallet, smart home controls, and app replies from the lock screen as well.

Step 2: Use Device Encryption and Auto-Wipe Features

Both iOS and Android devices support encryption, which protects your stored data even if someone removes the SIM or memory card. For iPhones, this is enabled by default once you set a passcode. For Android, check under Settings > Security > Encryption to ensure device and SD card encryption are active.

You can also set your phone to **erase itself after multiple failed passcode attempts**:

- On iPhone: Settings > Face ID & Passcode > "Erase Data" (after 10 failed attempts).
- On Android: Settings > Lock Screen > Secure Lock Settings (availability may vary by manufacturer).

Step 3: Act Immediately If Your Phone Is Lost or Stolen

If your phone disappears, don't wait—**act fast**:

1. **Use Find My iPhone or Find My Device** from another phone or desktop to locate it. If it shows up nearby, play a sound to help locate it. If not, immediately enable "Lost Mode" (iPhone) or "Secure Device" (Android), which locks the phone and displays a message with your contact info.

2. If recovery seems unlikely, use the **Remote Wipe** function to erase your data. This is a last resort but necessary if the device falls into the wrong hands.

3. **Change all important passwords**—especially for your email, banking apps, and social media. If someone gets into your email, they can reset everything else. Prioritize email and cloud services first.

4. **Contact your mobile carrier** to report the loss. They can disable your SIM card and prevent unauthorized calls or SIM swaps.

5. **Report the theft to local law enforcement**. Include the make, model, and IMEI number of your device (you can find this on the box or in your account

with your carrier). This may help in recovery or protect you from liability in case your phone is used for illegal activity.

Step 4: Protect Yourself from Seizure or Intrusion

In some situations—like traveling internationally, participating in protests, or facing legal investigations—your phone may be **seized by authorities** or border agents. If this is a concern, here are some steps to protect your privacy:

- Use **strong, non-biometric passcodes**. Biometric data (fingerprints, face scans) can sometimes be compelled by authorities, depending on local laws. A long alphanumeric passcode offers stronger legal and technical protection.

- Use apps like **Signal** that allow "sealed sender" messages and PIN locks, so even if someone accesses your phone, your messages remain encrypted and unreadable.

- Disable **cloud syncing for sensitive apps** temporarily before entering high-risk situations.

- Use a **secondary phone** with limited apps and data for travel or public demonstrations. Keep your primary device secured and stored safely.

Step 5: Post-Recovery Measures

If you recover your phone, perform a full **security audit**:

- Check for unauthorized access or changed settings.
- Review app permissions and login sessions for key accounts.
- Change all passwords stored on the phone.
- Reinstall your operating system or perform a factory reset if tampering is suspected.

Bonus: Record Your Device Details Now

Write down or securely store:

- IMEI number (dial *#06# to find it)
- Make and model
- Purchase receipt or serial number
- A recent backup (preferably encrypted)

These details can be invaluable in police reports, insurance claims, or proving ownership.

In summary, your phone can be your best friend—or your biggest liability. Taking proactive steps today could save you from legal, financial, or emotional distress tomorrow. The more security layers you add before a crisis, the fewer regrets you'll have afterward.

In the next chapter, we'll cover **mobile security for families and children**, including parental controls, safe browsing, and how to protect young users from inappropriate content and online predators.

Raj and his lost phone

Raj was on his way home from work, exhausted after a long day in the city. He hopped off the train, grabbed a slice of pizza, and didn't notice until he reached his apartment that something felt wrong. His heart sank when he realized his phone—his digital life—was gone. He checked every pocket, retraced his steps, and called it from his laptop. Nothing. It was either stolen or left on the train, and by now, probably long gone.

Panic set in. His phone contained everything—banking apps, two-factor authentication for work logins, personal photos, client contacts, and passwords saved in his browser. His mind raced: could someone access his email? His crypto wallet? His family photos?

Fortunately, Raj had listened to a cybersecurity podcast months ago and followed some of its advice. He raced to his computer and opened the Find My Device page. Within seconds, a green dot showed up on a map: his phone was still powered on and now appeared to be somewhere across town. Without hesitating, he locked the device remotely and added a custom message to the lock screen: “Lost phone. Please call 555-**** if found.”

But after thirty minutes, the phone stopped updating its location. It was either powered off—or wiped. Fearing the worst, Raj used the remote erase function. With one click, all his data was deleted from the phone.

He spent the rest of the evening changing his most important passwords—starting with email and cloud storage. Then came banking, social media, and finally, his encrypted messaging apps. He contacted his mobile carrier and had them disable the SIM. The representative explained that thieves often try to perform SIM swaps to gain access to texts and verification codes. That call might have saved him from financial disaster.

Still shaken, Raj filed a police report the next morning and provided the IMEI number from his phone’s packaging. The officer said they’d keep it on file in case the device showed up in a database.

But the real turning point came later that week. Raj read an article about how law enforcement or customs agents could legally seize your phone at borders without a warrant—and that in many countries, biometric unlocks could be compelled without your consent. He realized that while he had protected himself well from theft, he was still vulnerable in other ways.

Determined to improve, he bought a new phone and set it up more securely than ever before. He created a 12-digit alphanumeric passcode, disabled biometric unlocks, and limited lock screen notifications. He installed Signal and enabled disappearing messages. He disabled cloud backups for sensitive content and began keeping an encrypted offline backup on a secure drive at home. And for travel, he planned to carry a secondary "clean" phone with minimal apps and no sensitive content.

The experience changed his digital habits permanently. He used to treat his phone like a casual tool—something easily replaceable. But now, he understood it was more like his home or office: it contained the most private parts of his life and deserved the same level of protection.

Months later, Raj gave a talk at a small tech meetup about mobile security. He walked through what to do in the first 10 minutes after your phone is lost, what to set up in advance, and how to handle seizures at airports or borders. The audience was captivated. Many had never thought about these risks.

His final words stuck with everyone: "You lock your doors at night. You keep your wallet close. Why wouldn't you protect the one thing that holds everything about you—your phone?"

Chapter 9: Mobile Security for Families and Children

In today's connected world, mobile devices have become an integral part of family life. Children use smartphones and tablets for schoolwork, entertainment, and communication—often from a young age. While technology offers amazing benefits, it also opens the door to real digital dangers: online predators, inappropriate content, cyberbullying, addiction, data tracking, and privacy invasions. As a parent, guardian, or caregiver, securing your child's mobile experience is one of the most critical digital responsibilities you have.

Start by understanding the **threat landscape**. Children are not just passive users—they're active targets. Malicious apps, in-app purchases, social media algorithms, and even other children can exploit a young user's curiosity and naivety. Kids often don't realize the consequences of sharing personal information, clicking on ads, accepting friend requests, or downloading games that track their behavior.

The first and most important step is **open communication**. Children should understand that using a smartphone is a privilege that comes with responsibilities. Explain that online risks are real, just like physical ones—and that you're there to help, not spy. Framing the conversation around digital empowerment instead of surveillance creates trust and encourages honest dialogue when issues arise.

Next, implement **parental controls and age-appropriate restrictions**:

- On **iOS**, go to Settings > Screen Time. You can create a child profile, restrict app usage by age ratings, disable explicit content, block app installation, and limit screen time per category (games, social media, etc.).
- On **Android**, use the Family Link app. It allows you to set screen time limits, approve app downloads, block specific websites, and track usage.
- Enable **SafeSearch** on Google and YouTube. For younger children, consider apps like **YouTube Kids**, which filter content more aggressively.

Use a **child-safe browser** or a mobile security suite that includes parental web filters. Examples include **Qustodio**, **Norton Family**, **Bark**, or **Net Nanny**. These tools allow you to monitor what your child sees, block harmful content, and receive alerts about suspicious behavior—without reading their every text.

Teach your children about **data privacy** early. Explain why they should never share their full name, address, school, or photos with strangers. Help them understand what "tracking" means and how seemingly fun games can quietly collect location, contacts, and behavior to build profiles for advertising or worse.

Disable location tracking for most apps. Unless it's absolutely necessary (like for a family locator app), children's devices should not be broadcasting real-time GPS data. Also, turn off Bluetooth and AirDrop/Nearby Share unless needed, as these can be exploited to send unsolicited messages or files.

Discuss **cyberbullying and online harassment**. Make sure your child knows how to block and report users, and that it's always safe to talk to you if someone makes them uncomfortable online. Social media platforms like Instagram, Snapchat, and TikTok are often ground zero for inappropriate messaging or peer pressure.

Set clear **screen time expectations**. Studies show that excessive mobile use in children is linked to sleep disruption, reduced attention span, and anxiety. Establish screen-free zones (like bedrooms during bedtime or family meals) and consider setting downtime hours using built-in features.

Use **device management features** to monitor health, not control behavior. Apps that provide weekly usage summaries or app-by-app time reports can help kids understand and take ownership of their habits. Encouraging self-regulation is a powerful long-term lesson.

Back up the security setup with **strong physical protections** too:

- Use a robust password or biometric lock.
- Disable access to app stores or purchases without approval.
- Keep devices updated with the latest software patches.
- Store sensitive content (e.g., family documents or payment info) on separate, parent-controlled devices or accounts.

Finally, practice what you preach. Children learn most from observing. If you obsess over your phone or ignore privacy settings yourself, they're likely to follow suit. Share your own privacy habits, talk openly about mistakes, and make digital security a shared family value—not a one-time lecture.

In summary, the goal of mobile security for children isn't to isolate them from the online world, but to equip them with knowledge, boundaries, and habits that will protect them for life. As they grow, gradually grant them more autonomy—built on a foundation of trust, transparency, and tech wisdom.

In the final chapter, we'll explore **the future of mobile security and privacy**, including new technologies, evolving threats, and how to stay one step ahead in a world that's always online.

Why Monica installed family link

Monica was a single mom doing her best to balance work, parenting, and everything in between. Her 10-year-old son, Leo, had been asking for a smartphone for months. All his friends had one, and he wanted to play games, text his cousins, and watch videos after school. She resisted at first—but eventually, she caved in and bought him a basic Android phone with limited features.

At first, things went smoothly. Leo played a few math games, watched harmless YouTube videos, and sent emoji-filled texts to his grandparents. But within a few weeks, Monica started noticing changes. He stayed up later. He got upset when the phone was taken away. And one day, she overheard him on a video call with someone she didn't recognize.

She sat down with Leo that evening. “Who were you talking to?” she asked gently. He shrugged. “Just a guy I met on a game. He said he was 12.”

Her stomach turned. “What game?”

Leo opened the app. It was a multiplayer survival game she didn’t even know he had downloaded. When she checked the app permissions, she saw it had access to his microphone, location, and camera—and the chat feature allowed direct communication with anyone online.

Monica realized then that she had handed her son a tool that was more powerful—and more dangerous—than she’d thought. She needed help. That weekend, she reached out to a friend in IT who had children of his own. He walked her through a complete mobile safety setup.

They started by installing **Family Link** and locking down app downloads, screen time limits, and location sharing. Together, they uninstalled apps Leo didn’t need and reviewed every permission on the ones they kept. Then they set up **YouTube Kids** instead of regular YouTube and turned on **SafeSearch** in the browser.

They also had “the talk”—not just about strangers, but about privacy. Monica explained that not everyone online is who they say they are, and that no game is worth giving away your name, school, or photos. She told him she wasn't trying to spy on him, just protect him. Leo, to her surprise, actually appreciated it.

Later, they agreed on a simple rule: no screens in the bedroom after 8:00 p.m., and no new apps without her approval. She also started checking his weekly activity reports—not to punish, but to guide. When she saw he'd spent four hours on a single game one weekend, they had a conversation about balance and set new time limits together.

Over time, Leo adjusted. He stopped hiding his screen. He came to her when something weird happened in a group chat. And Monica became more confident in her own tech literacy. She wasn't a hacker, but she was now a proactive digital parent.

Months later, at a school meeting, Monica shared her experience with other parents. Many were shocked to learn how much access even children's apps requested. She showed them how to use parental controls, how to talk to kids about data privacy, and how to build trust rather than resentment around screen time rules.

The biggest shift wasn't in the technology—it was in the conversation. Monica no longer felt out of her depth, and Leo didn't feel like he was being policed. They had found a rhythm—one built on transparency, boundaries, and shared understanding.

As Leo got older, he started making smarter choices on his own. He began asking questions about new apps before downloading them, reviewing permissions, and even helping his younger cousin secure her tablet. Monica smiled. Her son wasn't just safer—he was becoming a digital citizen.

Chapter 10: The Future of Mobile Security — Trends, Threats, and How to Stay Ahead

Mobile security is no longer optional—it's a living, evolving necessity. As smartphones become more powerful and integrated into every aspect of our lives, the threats targeting them are becoming more sophisticated, persistent, and invisible. Understanding what's coming next is crucial to staying ahead of attackers, manipulative algorithms, and exploitative surveillance systems. In this final chapter, we'll explore future trends in mobile security, the threats you need to watch out for, and how to future-proof your digital life.

One of the biggest changes is the **rise of artificial intelligence (AI) in both attacks and defense**. Cybercriminals are now using AI to automate phishing attempts, generate hyper-realistic fake messages, and analyze behavioral patterns for more targeted exploits. Deepfake audio and video are emerging as powerful tools for impersonation, potentially tricking users into divulging sensitive information via what looks or sounds like a trusted source.

On the defense side, AI is also being used to power real-time threat detection, monitor anomalous behavior, and prevent data leaks before they occur. Tools like biometric authentication, behavior-based access control, and AI-powered firewalls will become standard features of mobile security suites. Expect your phone to become smarter at protecting itself—but also more reliant on data to do so.

Next, we'll see an increase in **zero-click attacks**. These are exploits that require no interaction from the user. A missed call, an incoming message, or simply receiving a file can trigger malware installation. These attacks often rely on previously undiscovered vulnerabilities (known as zero-days) in mobile operating systems or apps. While rare, they are extremely dangerous—especially for high-profile individuals, journalists, activists, and business leaders.

To defend against zero-click threats, always keep your device updated with the latest patches, disable unnecessary services like iMessage or FaceTime if not used, and limit exposure by using locked-down messaging platforms like Signal or apps that don't auto-load rich media.

Another major trend is the **expansion of mobile spyware and government surveillance tools**. Apps like Pegasus have shown the world just how easily even secured phones can be compromised by highly funded adversaries. As these tools become more affordable and accessible, they may be used not just by nation-states, but by stalkers, corporations, and bad actors in your personal or professional life.

The counter to this is increasing use of **secure hardware**—physical security keys, secure enclaves built into processors, and decentralized identity protocols. Phones like the Librem 5 and software like GrapheneOS are emerging to give users tighter control over their devices. Privacy-first alternatives to Google and Apple services will continue to gain traction, especially among users who want to reduce dependency on surveillance-based ecosystems.

Biometric evolution will also reshape mobile authentication. We're moving beyond fingerprints and facial recognition toward more passive biometrics—like behavioral biometrics (how you type, walk, or hold your phone), heartbeat recognition, and voiceprints. While these innovations promise stronger security, they also raise deeper ethical concerns about how much of ourselves we're giving away—and who gets to store and profit from that data.

Digital wallets and mobile IDs are also on the rise. From boarding passes and vaccine certificates to driver's licenses and crypto wallets, your phone will soon become your all-in-one identity. That means losing it, or having it compromised, becomes even more dangerous. Encrypted backups, physical 2FA devices, and offline recovery options will be critical safeguards in the years ahead.

Meanwhile, **5G and beyond** will bring faster, more stable connections—but also new attack surfaces. With more devices connected to mobile networks (smart appliances, vehicles, wearables), hackers will have more entry points. Expect to see a shift from app-based attacks to network-based ones, targeting not just your phone but the entire ecosystem around it.

So how do you future-proof your mobile security?

- **Stay educated**: Follow reputable cybersecurity blogs, podcasts, or newsletters. Threats evolve rapidly—so must your knowledge.

- **Reduce your digital footprint**: Limit app permissions, remove unused accounts, and delete data you no longer need.

- **Use layered security**: Biometric locks, encrypted messaging, VPNs, and security-focused browsers work best together.

- **Own your backups**: Keep offline, encrypted backups for essential data—don't rely solely on cloud providers.

- **Control your identity**: Be cautious about linking accounts, sharing real names or locations, and storing IDs on your phone.
- **Review settings quarterly**: Make mobile audits a habit. Reset advertising IDs, review app permissions, and update security apps.

The future of mobile security isn't about eliminating all risk—it's about making smart decisions, building strong habits, and staying proactive. In a world where the threats are silent and the attacks invisible, your awareness is your strongest defense.

In the final story chapter, we'll follow a family that learns how to build lasting mobile security habits—preparing not just for today's challenges, but for tomorrow's as well.

The spyware story

Julian and Maya were a tech-forward couple raising two kids in the suburbs of Denver. Their home was equipped with smart locks, voice assistants, security cameras, and every family member—even 8-year-old Ella—had their own device. They used phones for school, work, managing finances, and even opening their front door. Everything was synced, seamless, and convenient.

But a late-night documentary about spyware changed everything.

The show revealed how a journalist's phone had been hacked using a zero-click exploit. No taps. No downloads. Just one missed call—and the attacker had access to everything: camera, messages, contacts, and even encrypted apps. Julian sat frozen. He glanced at Maya. "If that can happen to him, what about us?"

They decided to run a digital audit.

Step one was checking software updates. Maya's phone hadn't updated in three months. Their daughter's iPad hadn't been patched in over a year. They quickly turned on auto-updates and checked every device in the house, including the Wi-Fi router.

Next came messaging. They had been using a mix of SMS, WhatsApp, and regular FaceTime. Julian switched the family to **Signal** and turned on disappearing messages. They also created a new habit: anything important or personal stayed off default channels. Signal was for family-only chats, and all backups were encrypted.

They added physical security keys to their main accounts—Google, iCloud, and banking. Ella's school account was now tied to a parent-managed email. They disabled biometric unlocks on their personal devices when traveling, choosing strong passcodes instead.

But the biggest eye-opener was the **advertising and tracking**. Their phones had been constantly broadcasting device IDs, search behaviors, and location history. Even when they weren't using the phone, apps were sending pings to servers across the world. They turned off ad personalization, disabled precise location access on everything except maps, and reset their advertising IDs.

Julian, who worked in finance, read more about upcoming threats. AI-driven phishing attacks. Fake video calls. Behavior-based tracking that could guess a user's identity based on how they typed or walked. He downloaded a privacy-focused browser, switched to a decentralized password manager, and started using a VPN daily. He began sharing updates at work, helping coworkers audit their own devices.

Maya focused on the kids. She installed a parental safety app with real-time alerts, locked app downloads, and set age-appropriate restrictions. But she didn't stop there. She taught Ella and her brother Liam about digital footprints, explaining how their actions today could affect future opportunities. They began asking questions before downloading games or sharing photos. Ella even helped a friend at school delete a sketchy app after hearing Maya's story.

By the end of the month, the family didn't feel afraid—they felt in control. Their phones were still useful, still fun, but no longer reckless. They knew how to lock down a device, spot a suspicious message, and talk about online risks without panic or shame.

Their takeaway was simple: **Security isn't a one-time setup—it's a way of thinking.** Like brushing your teeth or locking your door, digital hygiene became part of their routine.

A year later, nothing dramatic had happened. No hacks. No leaks. But that was the point. Quiet security meant peace of mind.

And while the world rushed toward smarter devices and more connected living, Julian and Maya knew they were ready—not because they had the latest tech, but because they had the right mindset.

They weren't just users anymore—they were guardians of their digital lives.

Security is not a destination—it's a practice

You've reached the end of this book, but your journey toward mobile security is just beginning.

We live in a world where our phones are more than just tools—they are digital extensions of ourselves. They know where we go, who we talk to, what we search, how we spend, and even what we think about when no one else is watching. And because they know so much, they must be protected with the same urgency, vigilance, and care we give to our homes, our families, and our identities.

Throughout this book, we've walked through every layer of mobile protection—from lock screen settings to encrypted messages, from app permission audits to spotting spyware and remote threats. You now understand that threats don't always look like threats. They often show up as convenience, free downloads, or default settings left untouched.

You also understand that the goal of security is not to create fear or paranoia—it's to create freedom. When you take control of your device, your data, and your digital habits, you move through the world with more confidence, clarity, and peace of mind.

You've learned how to:

- Harden your phone with smart default settings
- Choose the right messaging and video tools for true privacy
- Protect your photos, files, and cloud data from leaks and breaches
- Identify and remove malicious or manipulative apps
- Prepare for emergencies like theft, seizure, or device loss
- Guide your children and family through safe digital usage
- Stay ahead of future threats through habits, tools, and awareness

Most importantly, you've learned that **security is not a destination—it's a practice**. You'll need to revisit your settings, rethink your tools, and re-educate yourself as technology changes. What's secure today may not be tomorrow. But with the right mindset, you'll be prepared to adapt and thrive.

The Cyber Shield Academy series exists to help you do just that—to build real digital literacy in an age of distraction, manipulation, and hidden surveillance.

Thank you for committing to this knowledge. If you found this book helpful, share it with someone you care about. A friend. A parent. A teenager. A colleague. Digital security affects everyone—and by spreading awareness, you're not just protecting yourself. You're building a safer world for others, too.

Stay sharp. Stay private. And remember: **the power is in your pocket—but so is the risk. Protect both.**

www.ingramcontent.com/pod-product-compliance
Lightning Source LLC
LaVergne TN
LVHW022018200926
848481LV00007B/2451
9798349645112